THE LITTLE BOOK OF
Conflict
Transformation

D0038702

Published titles include:

The Little Book of Restorative Justice: Revised & Updated,
by Howard Zehr

The Little Book of Conflict Transformation,
by John Paul Lederach

The Little Book of Family Group Conferences, New-Zealand Style, by Allan MacRae and Howard Zehr

The Little Book of Strategic Peacebuilding, by Lisa Schirch

The Little Book of Strategic Negotiation,
by Jayne Seminare Docherty

The Little Book of Circle Processes, by Kay Pranis

The Little Book of Contemplative Photography, by Howard Zehr

The Little Book of Restorative Discipline for Schools,
by Lorraine Stutzman Amstutz and Judy H. Mullet

The Little Book of Trauma Healing, by Carolyn Yoder

The Little Book of Biblical Justice, by Chris Marshall

The Little Book of Restorative Justice for People in Prison,
by Barb Toews

The Little Book of Cool Tools for Hot Topics,
by Ron Kraybill and Evelyn Wright

El Pequeño Libro De Justicia Restaurativa, by Howard Zehr

The Little Book of Dialogue, by Lisa Schirch and David Campt

The Little Book of Victim Offender Conferencing,
by Lorraine Stutzman Amstutz

The Little Book of Restorative Justice for Sexual Abuse, by Judah Oudshoorn with Michelle Jackett and Lorraine Stutzman Amstutz

The Big Book of Restorative Justice: Three Classic Justice & Peacebuilding Books in One Volume, by Howard Zehr, Lorraine S. Amstutz, Allan Macrae, and Kay Pranis

The Little Book of Transformative Community Conferencing,
by David Anderson Hooker

The Little Book of Restorative Justice in Education,
by Katherine Evans and Dorothy Vaandering

The Little Books of Justice & Peacebuilding present, in highly accessible form, key concepts and practices from the fields of restorative justice, conflict transformation, and peacebuilding. Written by leaders in these fields, they are designed for practitioners, students, and anyone interested in justice, peace, and conflict resolution.

The Little Books of Justice & Peacebuilding series is a cooperative effort between the Center for Justice and Peacebuilding of Eastern Mennonite University and publisher Good Books.

THE LITTLE BOOK OF
Conflict
Transformation

JOHN PAUL LEDERACH

Good Books®

NEW YORK, NEW YORK

Acknowledgments

Writing a *Little Book* was much harder than it appears. I had help along the way. First, I want to extend a warm and deeply appreciative thank you to Howard Zehr for conceptu-al-izing this Little Book Series and encouraging my involvement. More importantly, he had the first crack at helping me move from a verbose text to one that got to the point. I appreciate the excellent editing and sharpening that this text received from Phyllis Pell-man Good. It would not read this well with-out her advice and suggestions. I had a great boost on the com-puter-generated graphics from my good friends at the Consor-tium on Conflict Resolution from the University of Colorado, particularly from Heidi and Guy Burgess. Of particular note, I had the wonderful opportunity of having the Master's students from the Kroc Institute's (Notre Dame) class of 2002-2003 read my first draft and spend a full day of class improving and clar-ifying the concepts. Their ideas and suggestions are found throughout.

I would like to extend a big note of gratitude to John and Gina Martin-Smith for the use of their house in Nederland, Colorado, where I got to watch the aspens turn from green to yellow at 8,500 feet as I wrote this text.

Finally, I recognize that none of my writing would take place without the patient support and encouragement of my family, especially Wendy, with whom I have had many coffees while discussing the ideas found in this book and how to say them better.

Cover photograph by Howard Zehr
Design by Dawn J. Ranck

THE LITTLE BOOK OF CONFLICT TRANSFORMATION

Good Books books may be purchased in bulk at special discounts for sales promotion, corporate gifts, fund-raising, or educational purposes. Special editions can also be created to specifications. For details, contact the Special Sales Department, Good Books, 307 West 36th Street, 11th Floor, New York, NY 10018 or info@skyhorsepublishing.com.

Good Books is an imprint of Skyhorse Publishing, Inc.®, a Delaware corporation.

Visit our website at www.goodbooks.com.

10 9 8 7 6 5 4

Library of Congress Cataloging-in-Publication Data

Lederach, John Paul.
The little book of conflict transformation / John Paul Lederach.
    p. cm.
Includes bibliographical references.
ISBN 1-56148-390-7; 978-1-56148-390-7
1. Conflict management. 2. Social conflict. I. Title.
HM1126.L43 2003
303.6'9--dc21
2003049110

Printed in Canada

Table of Contents

1.
Conflict Transformation?

Conflict *resolution* . . . conflict *management* . . . but conflict *transformation?*

I began using the term *conflict transformation* in the 1980s, after intensive experience in Central America caused me to re-examine the language of the field.

When I arrived there my vocabulary was filled with the usual terminology of conflict resolution and management. I soon found, though, that my Latin colleagues had questions, even suspicions, about what was meant by such concepts. For them, *resolution* carried with it a danger of co-optation, an attempt to get rid of conflict when people were raising important and legitimate issues. It was not clear that *resolution* left room for advocacy. In their experience, quick solutions to deep social-political problems usually meant lots of good words but no real change. "Conflicts happen for a reason," they would say. "Is this *resolution* idea just another way to cover up the changes that are really needed?"

Their concerns were consistent with my own experience and perspective. My deepest sense of vocation, and the framework that informs much of this book, arises from a faith context that is grounded in an Anabaptist/Mennonite religious-ethical framework. This perspective understands peace as embedded in justice. It emphasizes the importance of building right relationships and social structures through a radical respect for human rights and life. It advocates nonviolence as a way of life and work.

So the concerns of my Latin colleagues hit home. In my work of helping to find constructive responses to violent conflict in Central America and elsewhere, I became increasingly convinced that much of what I was doing was seeking constructive change. "Conflict transformation" seemed to convey this meaning better than conflict *resolution* or *management*.

Conflict is normal in human relationships, and conflict is a motor of change.

In the 1990s, when I helped found the Conflict Transformation Program at Eastern Mennonite University (EMU), we had extensive debates about titles and terms. *Resolution* was better known and was widely accepted in mainstream academic and political circles. *Transformation* seemed too value-laden for some, too idealistic for others, and too airy-fairy and new-age for still others. In the end, we stuck with the transformation terminology. We believed it was accurate and scientifically sound and that it provided a clear vision.

For me, *conflict transformation* is accurate because I am engaged in constructive change efforts that include, and go beyond, the resolution of specific problems. It is scientifically sound language because it is based on two verifiable realities: conflict is normal in human relationships, and conflict is a motor of change. *Transformation* provides a clear and important vision because it brings into focus the horizon toward which we journey—the building of healthy relationships and communities, locally and globally. This goal requires real change in our current ways of relating.

But the question remains, what does *transformation* really mean?

Over the past decade or so, the terminology of transformation has become increasingly common in both practitioner and academic circles. There are transformational approaches in mediation as well as in the broader discipline of peace and conflict studies. In fact, I am now part of two graduate academic programs that use this terminology, the Joan B. Kroc Institute for International Peace Studies at Notre Dame and the Conflict Transformation Program at EMU. In spite of this, conflict transformation is not as yet a school of thought. I do believe that conflict transformation is a comprehensive orientation or framework that ultimately may require a fundamental change in our way of thinking.

What follows is my understanding of this framework based on my reading, my practice, and my teaching over the past 15 years. This Little Book is not a definitive statement; my understanding constantly evolves, pushed by experiences of practice and teaching.

My understanding both parallels and converges from the work of other authors, although I am not able to explore all of those connections here. I do not want to imply that my particular view of transformation is superior to those who use the term differently or to those who prefer the term *resolution*. In this Little Book I mean to engage the creative tension between themes of resolution and transformation in order to sharpen understanding, not to discredit the work of those who prefer other terms.

My purpose here is to add a voice to the ongoing discussion, to the search for greater understanding in human relationships.

2.
The Lenses of Conflict Transformation

In everyday settings we often experience conflict as a disruption in the natural flow of our relationships. We notice or feel that something is not right. Suddenly we find ourselves more attentive to things we had taken for granted. The relationship becomes complicated, not as easy and smooth as it once was.

No longer do we take things at face value. Instead, we spend time and energy interpreting and re-interpreting what things mean. Our communication becomes difficult, requiring more intentional effort. We find it harder to really hear what others are saying—unless of course, they agree with us. We cannot easily comprehend what the other person is up to.

Our very physiology changes as our feelings translate from uneasiness to anxiety to even outright pain. In such a situation we often experience a growing sense of urgency leading to deeper and deeper frustration as the conflict progresses, especially if no end is in sight.

If someone uninvolved in the situation asks, "What is the conflict about?" we can translate our explanations into a kind of conflict "topography," a relief map of the peaks and valleys of our conflict. The peaks are what we see as the significant challenges in the conflict, often with an emphasis on the most recent, the one we are now climbing. Often we identify this mountain we are currently climbing as the primary issue or issues we are dealing with, the content of the conflict. The valleys represent failures, the inability to negotiate adequate solutions. And the whole of the mountain range—the overall picture of our relational patterns—often seems vague and distant, just as it is difficult to see the whole of a mountain range when you are climbing a specific peak.

This topographical conflict map illustrates our tendency to view conflict by focusing on the immediate "presenting" problems. We give our energy to reducing anxiety and pain by looking for a solution to the presenting problems without seeing the bigger map of the conflict itself. We also tend to view the conflict as a series of challenges and failures—peaks and valleys—without a real sense of the underlying causes and forces in the conflict.

The purpose of this book is to ask how a transformational approach addresses these tendencies and how that might be different from a conflict resolution or management perspective. What does conflict transformation look for and what does it see as the basis for developing a response to conflict?

As a starting point, let us explore the differences between the terms *look* and *see*. To look is to draw attention or to pay attention to something. In everyday language we often say, "Would you look over here please!" or

"Look at that!" In other words, looking requires lenses that draw attention and help us become aware. To see, on the other hand, is to look beyond and deeper. Seeing seeks insight and understanding. In everyday language we say, "Do you *see* what I mean?" Understanding is the process of creating meaning. Meaning requires that we bring something into sharper focus.

> *Conflict transformation*
>
> *is a way of*
>
> **looking** *as well as* **seeing.**

Conflict transformation is more than a set of specific techniques; it is a way of looking as well as seeing. Looking and seeing both require lenses. So conflict transformation suggests a set of lenses through which we view social conflict.

We might think of these lenses as a set of specialized eyeglasses. For the first time in my life, I am wearing progressive lenses; in these eyeglasses I have three different lens types within the same lens. Each has its own function. One lens or lens segment helps bring into focus things at a great distance that would otherwise be a blur. A second brings into clarity things that are mid-range, like the computer screen. The final one, the reading or magnifying lens, helps me read a book or thread a fish line through a hook. This lens metaphor suggests several implications for the transformational approach to understanding conflict.

First, if I try to use the reading segment of the lens to see at a distance, the lens is useless. Each lens or lens segment has its function, and that is to bring into focus a specific aspect of reality. When it brings that piece of reality into focus, other aspects blur. If you look through a camera with a telephoto lens or a microscope at a slide of bacteria, you find this happening in dramatic fashion: as one layer of reality is brought into focus other layers are blurred. The out-of-focus layers of reality are still present, but they are not clear. Likewise, the lenses we use to view conflict will clarify certain layers or aspects of reality while blurring others. We cannot expect a single lens to do more than it was intended to do, and we cannot assume that what it brings into focus is the whole picture.

Since no one lens is capable of bringing everything into focus, we need multiple lenses to see different aspects of a complex reality. This recalls the old adage, "If all you have is a hammer, all you see are nails." We cannot expect a single lens to bring into focus all of the dimensions and implications of a conflict.

My three lenses are held together in a single frame. Each lens is different, but each must be in relationship with the others if the various dimensions of reality are to be held together as a whole. I need each lens to see a particular portion of reality, and I need them to be in relationship to see the whole. This is the usefulness of finding lenses that help us address specific aspects of conflicts, while at the same time providing a means to envision the whole picture.

The whole picture is somewhat like a map: it helps us to see a broad set of items located in different places and to see how they might be connected. In this book I suggest three lenses that help create a map of the whole. First, we need a lens to see the *immediate situation*. Second, we need a lens to see beyond the presenting problems toward the deeper *patterns* of relationship, including the context in which the conflict finds expression. Third, we need a conceptual *framework* that holds these perspectives together, one that permits us to connect the presenting problems with the deeper relational patterns. Such a framework can provide an overall understanding of the conflict, while creating a platform to address both the presenting issues and the changes needed at the level of the deeper relational patterns.

> **The lenses of conflict transformation show**
> - *the immediate situation*
> - *underlying patterns and context*
> - *a conceptual framework*

Let me give an example. Our family at home sometimes has lively arguments over household tasks, like doing dishes. We can have some good fights that seem to come out of nowhere over something terribly mundane. The conflict focuses on something concrete and specific: that pile of dirty dishes. However, the energy evoked suggests something far deeper is at play. In fact, at stake in this dispute is much more than who will wash the dishes. We are negotiating the nature and quality of our relationship, our expectations of each other, our interpretations of our identity as individuals and as a family, our sense of self-worth and care for each other, and the nature of power and decision-making in our relationship. Yes, all that is in the pile of dirty dishes.

Those concerns are implicit in the questions we ask: "Who's washing them tonight? Who's washed them in the past? Who'll wash them in the future?" You see, it is not just a matter of dirty dishes. The dishes cause a struggle because they show us things about our relationship—if we can see beyond or behind the dishes to the underlying or ongoing patterns and issues.

We could just address the question, "So who does the dishes tonight?" If we find an answer, our problem is solved. And on many occasions, given the lack of time or interest in going deeper, that is exactly what we do: we identify a quick solution to a problem. However, that fast resolution does not probe the deeper significance of what is happening in our relationship and in our family. And if this deeper level remains untouched, it creates energy that crops up in the next episode of dirty dishes, the next pile of laundry, or those shoes that just lie there in the middle of the floor.

Conflict transformation lenses suggest we look beyond the dishes to see the context of the relationship that is involved, and then look back again at the pile. Not satisfied with a quick solution that may seem to solve the immediate problem, transformation seeks to create a framework to address the *content*, the *context*, and the *structure* of the relationship. Transformation as an approach aspires to create constructive change processes through conflict. Those processes provide opportunity to learn about patterns and to address relationship structures

---

Frameworks address

- *content*
- *context*
- *structure of relationships*

---

while providing concrete solutions to presenting issues. Facetious example? Yes, if all we see is dishes. No, if dishes are a window permitting us to look into life, growth, relationship, and understanding.

How do we create these lenses? We will begin by defining more clearly what we mean by the term conflict transformation. We will explore how that approach understands conflict and change. We shall return then to the more practical task of how to develop and apply a transformational framework to social conflict.

3.
Defining
Conflict Transformation

Ipropose the following definition:

> **Conflict transformation is** *to envision and respond*
> **to the** *ebb and flow* **of social conflict**
> **as** *life-giving opportunities*
> **for creating** *constructive change processes*
> **that** *reduce violence,*
> *increase justice*
> **in** *direct interaction and social structures,*
> **and respond to real-life problems**
> **in** *human relationships.*

The meaning and implications of this definition will
be easier to understand if we analyze the italicized components. Imagine conflict transformation as a person on
a journey, comprised of a head, heart, hands, and legs.

Head
The head refers to the conceptual view of conflict—
how we think about and therefore prepare to approach

conflict. In the head we find the attitudes, perceptions, and orientations that we bring to creative conflict transformation. Our definition uses the terms *envision and respond.*

Envision is active, a verb. It requires an intentional perspective and attitude, a willingness to create and nurture a horizon that provides direction and purpose.

A transformational perspective is built upon two foundations:

- *a capacity to envision* conflict positively, as a natural phenomenon that creates potential for constructive growth, and
- *a willingness to respond* in ways that maximize this potential for positive change.

A transformational approach recognizes that conflict is a normal and continuous dynamic within human relationships. Moreover, conflict brings with it the potential for constructive change. Positive change does not always happen, of course. As we all know too well, many times conflict results in long-standing cycles of hurt and destruction. But the key to transformation is a proactive bias toward seeing conflict as a potential catalyst for growth.

> **A transformational approach recognizes that conflict is a normal and continuous dynamic within human relationships.**

Respond suggests that vision must result in action, engaging the opportunity. The tilt is toward involvement. *Respond* recognizes that the deepest understanding comes from the learning process of real-life experience.

Both foundations—*envision and respond*—imply a certain level of "head" work. They represent the ways we think and orient ourselves as we approach the conflicts in our lives, relationships, and communities.

Ebb and flow: We often see conflict primarily in terms of its rise and fall, its escalation and de-escalation, its peaks and valleys. In fact, we often focus on a singular peak or valley, a particular iteration or repetition of a conflict episode. A transformational perspective, rather than looking at a single peak or valley, views the entire mountain range.

Perhaps it is helpful here to change our metaphor to one that is less static. Rather than narrowly focusing on the single wave rising and crashing on the shore, conflict transformation starts with an understanding of the greater patterns, the ebb and flow of energies, times, and even whole seasons, in the great sea of relationships.

The sea as a metaphor suggests that there is a rhythm and pattern to the movements in our relational lives. At times the sea movements are predictable, calm, even soothing. Periodically, events, seasons, and climates combine to create great sea changes that affect everything around them.

A transformational approach seeks to understand the particular episode of conflict not in isolation, but as embedded in the greater pattern. Change is understood both at the level of immediate presenting issues and that of broader patterns and issues. The sea is constantly moving, fluid, and dynamic. Yet at the same time it has shape and form and can have monumental purpose.

Heart

The heart is the center of life in the human body. Physically, it generates the pulse that sustains life. Figuratively, it is the center of our emotions, intuitions, and spiritual life. This is the place from which we go out and to which we return for guidance, sustenance, and direction. The heart provides a starting and a returning point. Two ideas form such a center for conflict transformation.

Human relationships: Biologists and physicists tell us that life itself is found less in the physical substance of things than in the less visible connections and relationships between them. Similarly, in conflict transformation relationships are central. Like the heart in the body, conflicts flow from and return to relationships.

Relationships have visible dimensions, but they also have dimensions that are less visible. To encourage the positive potential inherent in conflict, we must concentrate on the less visible dimensions of relationships, rather than concentrating exclusively on the content and substance of the fighting that is often much more visible. The issues over which people fight are important and require creative response. However, relationships represent a web of connections that form the larger context, the human eco-system from which particular issues arise and are given life.

To return for a moment to our sea image, if an individual wave represents the peak of issues visibly seen in the escalation of social conflict, relationships are the ebb and flow of the sea itself. Relationships—visible and invisible, immediate and long-term—are the heart of transformational processes.

Life-giving opportunities: The word *life-giving* applied to a conflict situation reminds us of several things. On one

> *Conflict is an opportunity, a gift.*

hand, the language suggests that life gives us conflict, that conflict is a natural part of human experience. On the other, it assumes that conflict creates life like the pulsating heart of the body creates rhythmic blood flow which keeps us alive and moving.

Conflict flows from life. As I have emphasized above, rather than seeing conflict as a threat, we can understand it as providing opportunities to grow and to increase understanding of ourselves, of others, of our social structures. Conflicts in relationships at all levels are the way life helps us to stop, assess, and take notice. One way to truly know our humanness is to recognize the gift of conflict in our lives. Without it, life would be a monotonously flat topography of sameness and our relationships would be woefully superficial.

Conflict also creates life: through conflict we respond, innovate, and change. Conflict can be understood as the motor of change, that which keeps relationships and social structures honest, alive, and dynamically responsive to human needs, aspirations, and growth.

Hands

We refer to our hands as that part of the body capable of building things, able to touch, feel and affect the shape that things take. Hands bring us close to practice. When we say "hands-on," we mean that we are close to where the work takes place. Two terms of our definition stand out in this regard.

Constructive: Constructive can have two meanings. First, at its root it is a verb: to build, shape, and form.

Second, it is an adjective: to be a positive force. Transformation contains both these ideas. It seeks to understand, not negate or avoid, the reality that social conflict often develops violent and destructive patterns. Conflict transformation pursues the development of change processes which explicitly focus on creating positives from the difficult or negative. It encourages greater understanding of underlying relational and structural patterns while building creative solutions that improve relationships. Its bias is that this is possible, that conflict is opportunity.

Change processes: Central to this approach are *change processes,* the transformational component and the foundation of how conflict can move from being destructive toward being constructive. This movement can only be done by cultivating the capacity to see, understand, and respond to the presenting issues in the context of relationships and ongoing change processes. What are the processes that the conflict itself has generated? How can these processes be altered, or other processes initiated, that will move the conflict in a constructive direction? A focus on process is key to conflict transformation.

Conflict transformation focuses on the dynamic aspects of social conflict. At the hub of the transformational approach is a convergence of the relational context, a view of conflict-as-opportunity, and the encouragement of creative change processes. This approach includes, but is not driven by, an episodic view of conflict. Conflict is viewed within the flow and the web of relationships. As we shall see, a transformational lens sees the generation of creative "platforms" as the mechanism to address specific issues, while also working to change social structures and patterns.

Legs and Feet

Legs and feet represent the place where we touch the ground, where all our journeys hit the road. Like the hands, this is a point of action, where thought and heartbeat translate into response, direction, and momentum. Conflict transformation will be only utopian if it is unable to be responsive to real-life challenges, needs, and realities.

Rather than seeing peace as a static "end-state," conflict transformation views peace as a continuously evolving and developing quality of relationship.

A transformational view engages two paradoxes as the place where action is pursued and raises these questions: How do we address conflict in ways that reduce violence and increase justice in human relationships? And how do we develop a capacity for constructive, direct, face-to-face interaction and, at the same time, address systemic and structural changes?

Reduce violence and increase justice: Conflict transformation views peace as centered and rooted in the quality of relationships. These relationships have two dimensions: our face-to-face interactions and the ways we structure our social, political, economic, and cultural relationships. In this sense, peace is what the New Sciences[1] call a "process-structure": a phenomenon that is simultaneously dynamic, adaptive, and changing, and yet has a form, purpose, and direction that gives it shape. Rather than seeing peace as a static "end-state," conflict transformation views peace as a continuously evolving and developing quality of relationships. Peace work, therefore, is characterized by intentional efforts to address the natural ebb and flow of human conflict through nonviolent approaches, which address issues and increase understanding, equality, and respect in relationships.

To reduce violence requires that we address the presenting issues and content of an episode of conflict, and also its underlying patterns and causes. This requires us to address justice issues. While we do that, we must proceed in an equitable way toward substantive change. People must have access and voice in decisions that affect their lives. In addition, the patterns that create injustice must be addressed and changed at both relational and structural levels.

Direct interaction and social structures: As suggested above, we need to develop capacities to envision and engage in change processes at all levels of relationships: interpersonal, inter-group, and social-structural. One set of capacities points toward direct, face-to-face interaction. The other set underscores the need to see, pursue, and create change in our ways of organizing social structures, from families to complex bureaucracies, from the local to the global.

Conflict transformation suggests that a fundamental way to promote constructive change on all these levels is dialogue. Dialogue is essential to justice and peace on both an interpersonal and a structural level. It is not the only mechanism, but it is an essential one.

We typically think of dialogue as direct interaction between people or groups. Conflict transformation shares this view. Many of the skill-based mechanisms that are called upon to reduce violence are rooted in the communicative abilities to exchange ideas, find common definitions to issues, and seek ways forward toward solutions.

> *Conflict transformation is*
> *to envision and respond to the ebb and flow*
> *of social conflict as life-giving opportunities*
> *for creating constructive change processes*
> *that reduce violence,*
> *increase justice in direct interaction*
> *and social structures,*
> *and respond to real-life problems*
> *in human relationships.*

However, a transformational view believes that dialogue is necessary for both creating and addressing social and public spheres where human institutions, structures, and patterns of relationships are constructed. Processes and spaces must be created so that people can engage and shape the structures that order their community life, broadly defined. Dialogue is needed to provide access to, a voice in, and constructive interaction with, the ways we formalize our relationships and in the ways our organizations and structures are built, respond, and behave.

At its heart, conflict transformation focuses on creating adaptive responses to human conflict through change processes which increase justice and reduce violence.

4.
Conflict and Change

Conflict happens. It is normal and it is continuously present in human relationships. Change happens as well. Human community and relationships are not static but ever dynamic, adapting, changing.

Conflict impacts situations and changes things in many different ways. We can analyze these changes in four broad categories: the *personal*, the *relational*, the *structural*, and the *cultural*.

Conflict impacts us

personally,

relationally,

structurally,

culturally.

We can also think about these changes in response to two questions.

- *What changes are occurring* as a result of conflict? For example, what are the patterns and the effects of this conflict?

- *What kind of changes do we seek?* To answer this second question, we need to ask what our values and intentions may be.

With these two questions in mind, let us consider these four areas.

The *personal* aspect of conflict refers to changes affected in and desired for the individual. This involves the full person, including the cognitive, emotional, perceptual, and spiritual dimensions.

From a descriptive perspective, transformation reminds us that we as individuals are affected by conflict in both negative and positive ways. Conflict affects our physical well-being, self-esteem, emotional stability, capacity to perceive accurately, and spiritual integrity.

> **Change must be viewed descriptively and prescriptively.**

Prescriptively, transformation represents deliberate intervention to minimize the destructive effects of social conflict and to maximize its potential for growth in the person as an individual human being, at physical, emotional, and spiritual levels.

The *relational* dimension represents changes in face-to-face relationships. Here we consider relational affectivity, power, and interdependence, and the expressive, communicative, and interactive aspects of conflict.

Descriptively, transformation refers to how the *patterns* of communication and interaction are affected by conflict. It looks beyond the tension around the visible issues to the underlying changes produced by conflict; this includes patterns of how people perceive, what they desire, what they pursue, and how they structure their relationships interpersonally, as well as inter-group and intra-group. Conflict changes relationships. It raises to a more explicit level questions such as these: How close or distant do people wish to be in their relationships? How will they use, build, and share power? How do they perceive themselves, each other, and their expectations? What are their hopes and fears for their lives and relationships, their patterns of communication and interaction?

Prescriptively, transformation represents intervening intentionally to minimize poorly functioning communication and to maximize mutual understanding. This includes trying to bring to the surface explicitly the relational fears, hopes, and goals of the people involved.

The *structural* dimension highlights the underlying causes of conflict and the patterns and changes it brings about in social, political, and economic structures. This aspect focuses attention on how social structures, organizations, and institutions are built, sustained, and changed by conflict. It is about the ways people build and organize social, economic, political, and institutional relationships to meet basic human needs, provide access to resources, and make decisions that affect groups, communities, and whole societies.

Transformation at the descriptive level involves analyzing the social conditions that give rise to conflict and the way that conflict affects change in the existing social structures and patterns of making decisions.

At a prescriptive level transformation represents deliberately intervening in order to gain insight into the underlying causes and social conditions which create and foster violent expressions of conflict. In addition, it openly promotes nonviolent means to reduce adversarial interaction and seeks to minimize—and ultimately eliminate—violence. (This includes nonviolent advocacy for change.) Pursuing such change promotes developing structures that meet basic human needs (substantive justice) while maximizing the involvement of people in decisions that affect them (procedural justice).

The *cultural* dimension refers to changes produced by conflict in the broadest patterns of group life, including identity, and the ways that culture affects patterns of response and conflict.

At a descriptive level, transformation attempts to understand how conflict affects and changes the cultural patterns of a group, and how those accumulated and shared patterns affect the way people in a given setting understand and respond to conflict.

Prescriptively, transformation seeks to help those in conflict to understand the cultural patterns that contribute to conflict in their setting, and then to identify, promote, and build on the resources and mechanisms within that culture for constructively responding to and handling conflict.

As an *analytical framework*, then, transformation seeks to understand social conflict as it emerges from and produces changes in the personal, relational, structural, and cultural dimensions of human experience. As an *intervening strategy*, transformation works to promote constructive processes with the following range of change-oriented goals.

Change Goals in Conflict Tranformation

Personal

- Minimize destructive effects of social conflict and maximize the potential for growth and well-being in the person as an individual human being at physical, emotional, intellectual, and spiritual levels.

Relational

- Minimize poorly functioning communication and maximize understanding.
- Bring out and work with fears and hopes related to emotions and interdependence in the relationship.

Structural

- Understand and address root causes and social conditions that give rise to violent and other harmful expressions of conflict.
- Promote nonviolent mechanisms that reduce adversarial confrontation and that minimize and ultimately eliminate violence.
- Foster the development of structures to meet basic human needs (substantive justice) and to maximize participation of people in decisions that affect their lives (procedural justice).

Cultural

- Identify and understand the cultural patterns that contribute to the rise of violent expressions of conflict.
- Identify and build upon resources and mechanisms within a cultural setting for constructively responding to and handling conflict.

5.
Connecting Resolution and Transformation

We have explored transformation as a perspective on conflict and change. How, then, do the ideas become applicable? We cannot leave the conceptual level completely as we move toward the practical. We must develop an image of our purpose—the "big picture."

Using other terms, we need a strategic vision in order to assess and develop specific plans and responses. The big picture helps us see purpose and direction. Without it, we can easily find ourselves responding to a myriad of issues, crises, and energy-filled anxieties. We may end up moving with a great sense of urgency but without a clear understanding of what our responses add up to. We may solve lots of immediate problems without necessarily creating any significant constructive social change.

Part of creating the big picture is identifying and analyzing our guiding metaphors. A good place to start is by comparing the metaphors of resolution and transformation.

I have said that *conflict transformation* provides a perspective on conflict that is different than that of *conflict resolution*. I believe this is a reorientation so fundamental that it changes the very way we look at and respond to social conflict. We must analyze this because of its implications for practice.

To move toward *transformation* and away from *resolution* means we are changing or expanding our guiding idea. The language of *resolution* has until now largely provided the framing structure for our interpretations and actions.

Conflict resolution is a well-known and widely accepted term in both practitioner and research communities. It has defined a field for more than a half a century. Within that field are many approaches, understandings, and definitions, some of which are close to the way I am defining a transformational perspective. However, in this particular discussion I am not so interested in the definitions of resolution and transformation as terms. I am interested in the meaning or implications suggested by the ideas they represent.

At its most basic, the language of resolution implies finding a solution to a problem. It guides our thinking toward bringing some set of events or issues, usually experienced as very painful, to an end. There is a definitiveness and finality created in the language when we add "re" to "solution:" We seek a conclusion. *Resolution's* guiding question is this: How do we end something that is not desired?

Transformation directs us toward change, to how things move from one shape to a different one. The change process is fundamental to this guiding language. By its nature, when we add "trans" to "form" we must contemplate both the presenting situation and a new one. *Transformation's* guiding question is this: How do we end something not desired and build something we do desire?

Resolution often focuses our attention on the presenting problems. Given its emphasis on immediate solutions, it tends to concentrate on the substance and content of the problem. This may explain why there has been such a predominance of literature on negotiation technique within the field of conflict resolution—from popular airport bookstands to the halls of major research institutes. In short, resolution is content-centered.

Transformation, on the other hand, includes the concern for content, but centers its attention on the *context* of relationship patterns. It sees conflict as embedded in the web and system of relational patterns.

> *Transformation's guiding question is this: How do we end something not desired and build something we do desire?*

We can take this a step further. Both resolution and transformation claim to be process-oriented. Resolution, however, sees the development of process as centered on the immediacy of the relationship where the symptoms of crisis and disruption take place. Transformation envisions the presenting problem as an opportunity to engage a broader context, to explore and understand the system of relationships and patterns that gave birth to the crisis. It seeks to address both the immediate issues and the system of relational patterns.

This requires longer-term vision that goes beyond the anxieties of immediate needs. Transformation actively pursues a crisis-responsive approach rather than one that is crisis-*driven*. The impulse to *resolve* leads toward providing short-term relief to pain and anxiety by negotiating answers to presenting problems. Those answers may or may not deal with the deeper context and patterns of relationships which caused the problems.

Finally, each perspective has an accompanying view of conflict. Resolution has tended to focus primarily on methods for de-escalating. Transformation involves both de-escalating and engaging conflict, even escalating in pursuit of constructive change. Constructive change requires a variety of roles, functions, and processes, some of which may push conflict out into the open.

In summary, transformation includes, but is not bound by, the contributions and approaches proposed by resolution-based language. It goes beyond a process focused on the resolution of a particular problem or *episode* of conflict to seek the *epicenter* of conflict.

An *episode* of conflict is the visible expression of conflict rising within the relationship or system, usually within a distinct time frame. It generates attention and energy around a particular set of issues that need response. The *epicenter* of conflict is the web of relational patterns, often providing a history of lived episodes, from which new episodes and issues emerge. If the episode releases conflict energy in the relationship, the epicenter is where the energy is produced.

> *Transformation*
> *addresses both the episode*
> *and the epicenter*
> *of conflict.*

A focus on the epicenter provides a core set of questions. What is the bigger picture of relationships and patterns within which the problem rises? What are the potential and needed change processes that can respond to the immediate issues, as well as the broader setting that creates the crisis? What longer-term vision can we hope to build from the seeds and potential in the current crisis?

The idea of transformation offers an expanded view of time. It situates issues and crises within a framework of relationships and social context. It creates a lens for viewing both solutions and ongoing change processes. The key to creative solutions, transformation suggests, lies in designing a responsive and adaptive platform for constructive change that is made possible by the crisis and the presenting issues. The episode of conflict becomes an opportunity to address the epicenter of conflict.

	Conflict Resolution Perspective	Conflict Transformation Perspective
The key question	How do we end something not desired?	How do we end something destructive and build something desired?
The focus	It is content-centered.	It is relationship-centered.
The purpose	To achieve an agreement and solution to the presenting problem creating the crisis.	To promote constructive change processes, inclusive of, but not limited to, immediate solutions.
The development of the process	It is embedded and built around the immediacy of the relationship where the symptoms of disruptions appear.	It envisions the presenting problem as an opportunity for response to symptoms **and** engagement of systems within which relationships are embedded.
Time frame	The horizon is short-term relief to pain, anxiety, and difficulties.	The horizon for change is mid- to long-range and is intentionally crisis-responsive rather than crisis-driven.
View of conflict	It envisions the need to de-escalate conflict processes.	It envisions conflict as an ecology that is relationally dynamic with ebb (conflict de-escalation to pursue constructive change) and flow (conflict escalation to pursue constructive change).

Conflict Resolution and Conflict Transformation: A Brief Comparison of Perspective

6.
Creating a Map
of Conflict

The "big picture" of conflict transformation suggested in the previous chapter can be visualized as a map or diagram (Figure 1). It is comprised of three main components, each representing a point of inquiry in the development of strategy and response to conflict. We begin with the first point of inquiry, the Presenting Situation.

Inquiry 1:

The presenting situation

Figure 1 visualizes the Presenting Situation as a set of embedded spheres shown here as ellipses. A sphere is a useful metaphor that helps us think about spaces of exploration, meaning, and action. As opposed to a circle, a sphere has somewhat looser boundaries, as in the phrase, "a sphere of activity." A sphere invites us into an evolving space.

Here the sphere of immediate issues is embedded in the sphere of patterns, which in turn is embedded in the sphere of history. This reminds us that the immediate issues are rooted in a context—in patterns of relationships and structures, all with a history.

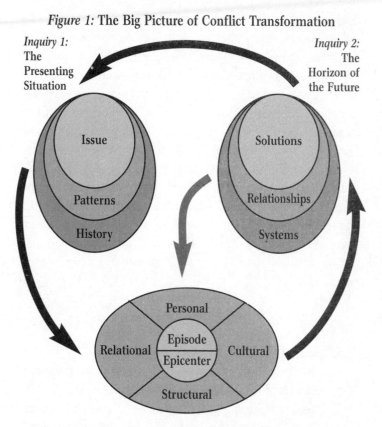

Figure 1: The Big Picture of Conflict Transformation

Inquiry 1: The Presenting Situation

Inquiry 2: The Horizon of the Future

Issue

Patterns

History

Solutions

Relationships

Systems

Personal

Relational

Episode

Epicenter

Cultural

Structural

Inquiry 3: The Development of Change Processes

A key paradox of the presenting issues is the connection between the present and the past. The patterns of "how things have been" provide the context from which the immediate issues of dispute rise to the surface. The presenting issues create opportunity to remember and recognize, but presenting issues do not in themselves have the power to positively change what has already transpired. The potential for constructive change lies in our ability to recognize, understand, and redress what has happened. Positive change requires a willingness to create new ways of interacting, to build relationships and structures that look toward the future.

To return to our definition, the immediacy of the presenting issues, and the energy released as people contend over these issues, defines the "episodic" expression of the conflict. Moving through the presenting issues toward the spheres of relational and historical patterns takes us to the epicenter of conflict, which is always capable of regenerating new episodes, either on similar or on different issues. Transformation seeks to see and understand both: the episode and the epicenter. This takes us to another level of inquiry—Inquiry Three—but first we need to examine another set of embedded spheres, the horizon of the future.

Inquiry 2:
The horizon of the future

The second point of inquiry helps us think about the horizon of the future. The image of a horizon may be an appropriate way to imagine the future. A horizon can be seen but not touched. It can provide orientation, but it requires constant journeying each day. The future is something we can visualize but do not control.

In our big picture the future is represented as a set of spheres and is meant to suggest an open and dynamically evolving future. Embedded in this space of engagement and exploration are smaller spheres—immediate solutions, relationships, structures—that involve possible avenues for dealing with the immediate presenting issues, as well as processes that address relational and structural patterns. The inquiry into the horizon of the future brings forward questions like these: What do we hope to build? What would we ideally like to see in place? How can we address all levels—immediate solutions as well as underlying patterns of relationships and structures?

If these two sets of spheres or levels of inquiry (the presenting situation and the horizon of the future) were the only components of the big picture, we might have a model of linear change: a movement from the present situation to the desired future. However, it is important to visualize the overall picture as an interconnected circle. We can see this in the energies depicted by the arrows. The presenting situation spheres create a push to do something about these issues. They are a kind of social energy creating an impulse toward change, depicted as the arrow moving forward. On the other side, the horizon of the future harnesses an impulse that points toward possibilities of what could be constructed and built. The horizon represents a social energy that informs and creates orientation. Here the arrow points both back toward the immediate situation and forward to the range of change processes that may emerge. The combination of arrows provides an overall circle. In other words, our big picture is both a circular and a linear process, or what we earlier referred to as a process-structure.

Inquiry 3:
The development of change processes

This brings us to the third major inquiry, the design and support of change processes. Again, we can visualize these in the form of a sphere with embedded components. This overall sphere requires that we think about response to conflict as the development of processes of change that attend to the web of interconnected needs, relationships, and patterns on all four levels: personal, relational, cultural, and structural.

Note that we describe "processes" in the plural. Processes of change require us to hold together at the same time multiple interdependent initiatives that are different but not incompatible. Transformation requires us to reflect on multiple levels and types of change processes, rather than addressing ourselves only to a single operational solution. The change processes address both the episodic content and the patterns and context or epicenter. We must conceptualize multiple change processes that address solutions for immediate problems and *at the same time* processes that create a platform for longer-term change of relational and structural patterns.

This approach goes beyond negotiating solutions and builds toward something new.

In the broadest terms, then, the transformation framework comprises three inquiries: the presenting situation, the horizon of preferred future, and the development of change processes linking the two. The movement from the present toward the desired future is not a straight line. Rather, it represents a dynamic set of initiatives that set in motion change processes and promote long-term change strategies, while providing responses to specific, immediate needs. Conflict transformation faces these challenges: What kind of changes and solutions are needed? At what levels? Around which issues? Embedded in which relationships?

Such a framework emphasizes the challenge of how to *end* something not desired and how to *build* something that is desired. Remember, this approach connects resolution practices that have often looked for ways to end a particular "iteration" or repetition of conflict with a transformation orientation that works at building ongoing change at relational and structural levels. On the one hand, this framework deals with presenting problems and the content of the conflict, seeking to find mutually acceptable solutions to both. These are often processes that reduce violence and the continued escalation of conflict. On the other hand, this approach goes beyond negotiating solutions and builds toward something new. This requires the negotiation of change processes rising from a broader understanding of relational patterns and historical context.

Transformation negotiates both solutions and social change initiatives. It requires a capacity to see through and beyond the presenting issues to the deeper patterns, while seeking creative responses that address real-life issues in real time. However, to more fully comprehend this approach we need to understand more completely how platforms for constructive change are conceptualized and developed as process-structures.

7.
Process-Structures
as Platforms
for Change

With our conceptual map or diagram in mind, we must now consider how transformation actually operates. Our key challenge is this: how to develop and sustain a platform or strategic plan that has a capacity to adapt and generate ongoing desired change, while at the same responding creatively to immediate needs. We can do this by thinking about platforms as process-structures.

In the New Sciences, process-structures are described as natural phenomena that are dynamic, adaptive, and changing, while at the same time maintaining a functional and recognizable form and structure. Margaret Wheatley refers to them as "things that maintain form over time yet have no rigidity of structure."[2] They are also, paradoxically, phenomena which are both circular and linear. By making these two terms—"process" and "structure"—into a single hyphenated word, we emphasize the reality that in a single concept we combine two interdependent characteristics: adaptability and purpose.

Conflict transformation envisions conflict and our response to conflict as the creation of processes having these two characteristics. Change itself has the feel of a process-structure. We are reminded to explore more closely how we might understand the differences and contributions of circles and lines.

Both circular and linear

Circular means things go around. Sometimes the word *circular* has a negative implication, as in *circular thinking*. *Circular* also has positive implications. First, it reminds us that things are connected and in relationship. Second, it suggests that the growth of something often nourishes itself from its own process and dynamic. Third, and most critical to our inquiry, the concept of circularity reminds us that processes of change are not one-directional. This is particularly important to keep in mind as we experience the ebb and flow of our efforts to create platforms for constructive response.

Circularity suggests that we need to think carefully about how social change actually happens. Often we look at change through a rear-view mirror, observing the pattern of how something got from one place to another. But, when we are in the middle of change, and when we are looking forward toward what can be done, the process of change never seems clear or neat. The circle reminds us that change is not evenly paced, nor is it one-directional.

The circle of change

We can begin by placing the circle in chronological time (see Figure 2). To do this, I have found it useful to pay attention to what change actually feels like, especially when the persons involved care deeply about certain kinds of social change or are in the middle of a difficult conflict. Figure 2 identifies four common experiences, each very different, each wrapped up with the other, each part of the circle of change.

Sometimes we feel as if desired change is happening, as if there is progress. Things are moving forward in a desired direction, toward the goals or aspirations we hold for ourselves and our relationships.

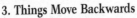

Figure 2: **Change as a Circle**

3. Things Move Backwards

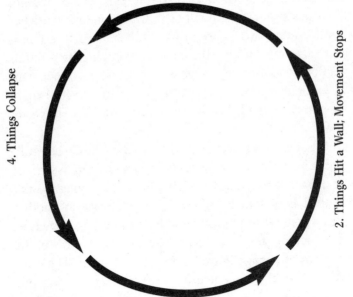

4. Things Collapse

2. Things Hit a Wall; Movement Stops

1. Things Move Forward

At other times we feel as if we have reached an impasse. A wall has been erected that blocks and stops everything.

Then there are times when the change processes seem to be going backwards. We feel as if what has been achieved is now being undone. We hear language like, "In a single stroke, years of work have been set back." We experience "swimming against the tide" or "heading upstream." These metaphors underscore the reality that change—even positive change—includes periods of going backward as much as going forward.

Then there are times when we feel as though we are living through a complete breakdown. Things are not just retrogressing. Instead, they are coming apart, collapsing like a building falling. In the ebb and flow of conflict and peacebuilding we experience these periods as deeply depressing, often accompanied by a phrase such as, "We have to start from ground zero."

All these experiences, though not always in the same chronological order, are normal parts of the change circle. Understanding change as circular helps us to know and anticipate this. The circle recognizes that no one point in time determines the broader pattern. Rather, change encompasses different sets of patterns and directions as part of the whole.

The circle cautions us at each step: going forward too quickly may not be wise. Meeting an obstacle probably provides a useful reality check. Going backward may create more innovative ways forward. And coming down may create opportunities to build in wholly new ways.

At every step, circular thinking makes a practical appeal: Look. See. Adapt. It reminds us that change, like life, is never static. This is the circle portion of a dynamic process-structure.

The linear quality of change, on the other hand, means that things move from one point to the next. In mathematics, a line is the shortest route between two points. It is straight with no contours or detours. A linear orientation is associated with rational thinking, understanding things purely in terms of logical cause and effect. So how does this relate to that characteristic of change which we have just described as not one-directional or not logical in a pure sense? Recognizing the linear nature of change requires us to think about its overall direction and purpose. It is another—and essential—way of seeing the web of patterns of different factors relating and moving toward make a whole.

A linear view suggests that social forces move in broad directions, not usually visible to the naked eye, rarely obvious in short time frames. A linear perspective asks us to stand back and take a look at the overall direction of social conflict and the change we seek that includes history and future. Specifically, it requires us to look at the pattern of circles, not just the immediate experience.

Change as process-structure

Figure 3 graphically displays a simple process-structure. This picture holds together a web of dynamic circles creating an overall momentum and direction. Some might refer to this as a rotini, a spiral made up of multi-directional internal patterns that create a common overall movement.

Figure 3: A Simple Process-Structure

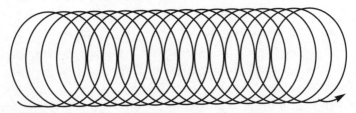

In the scientific community, opponents of linear thinking argue that linearity assumes a deterministic view of change which discourages our ability to predict and control outcomes. While this is a useful warning, I do not believe that a lack of control and determinism are incompatible with purpose and orientation. We have to seek "our North," as the Spanish would say; we must articulate how we think change actually happens and what direction it is going. This is the gift of seeing in a linear fashion: it requires us to articulate how we think things are related, how movement is created, and in what overall direction things are flowing. In other words, a linear approach pushes us to express and test our theories of change that too often lie unexplored and dormant beneath layers of rhetoric and our kneejerk responses and actions. Linear thinking says, "Hey, good intentions are not enough. How exactly is this action creating change? What is changing and in what direction is it going?" The key to creating a platform for transformation in the midst of conflict lies in holding together a healthy dose of both circular and linear perspectives.

Transformational platforms

A transformational approach requires us to build an ongoing and adaptive base at the epicenter of conflict, a "platform." A platform is like a scaffold-trampoline: it gives a base to stand on and jump from. The platform includes an understanding of the various levels of the conflict (the "big picture"), processes for addressing immediate problems and conflicts, a vision for the future, and a plan for change processes which will move in that direction. From this base it becomes possible to generate processes that create solutions to short-term needs and, at the same time, work on strategic, long-term, constructive change in systems and relationships.

Figure 4 presents this idea by adding to our process-structure (Figure 3) the escalation of conflict episodes, with the platform underlining it all. The process-structure spiral can be seen as the epicenter of the conflict, and the peaks or waves of the conflict as the episodes. The general rise and fall of the conflict and change processes provide an ongoing base from which processes can be generated. The escalation of conflict creates opportunity to establish and sustain this base. From the transformational view, developing a process to provide a solution to these immediate conflicts or problems is important, but not the key. More important in the long run is generating processes that: 1) provide adaptive responses to the immediate and future repetition of conflict episodes; and 2) address the deeper and longer-term re-

Figure 4: Transformational Platform

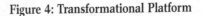
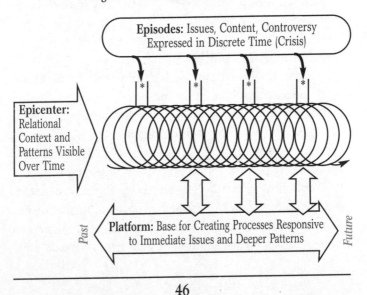

lational and systemic patterns that produce violent, destructive expressions of conflict.

A conflict transformation platform must be short-term responsive and long-term strategic. It must have the capacity to generate and regenerate change processes responsive to both episodes and the context or epicenter. Because of its dynamism and complexity, the platform is a process-structure, not just a process and not just a structure. A transformation platform must be adaptive, for it understands that conflict and change are constant, but the specific solutions and the forms they take are ephemeral.

Conflict transformation is a circular journey with a purpose. Undertaking this journey requires preparation.

8.
Developing
Our Capacities

As I have moved from thinking conceptually about conflict transformation to applying it, I have found it important to cultivate the following personal practices:

Practice 1:
Develop a capacity to see
presenting issues as a window

A transformational approach requires that we develop a capacity to see the immediate situation without being captivated, overwhelmed, or driven by the demands of presenting issues. It requires an ability to avoid the urgency that pushes for a quick solution and the anxieties that often accompany a system of relationships as conflict escalates.

The key to this practice requires these disciplines: 1) the ability to look and see beyond the presenting issues; 2) an empathy that allows one to understand the situation of another (person or group) but not to be drawn into the spin of their anxieties and fears; and 3) a capacity to create avenues of response that take seriously the presenting issues but are not driven by the need for quick solutions.

How do we do this? One way is to envision the presenting issues as a window. Windows are important in themselves, but once they are in place we rarely look at the window. We look through the glass, focusing our attention on what lies beyond the window. Likewise in conflict transformation we do not focus primary attention on the issues themselves in order to seek an apparent rapid solution. Rather, we look through the issue to bring into focus the scene that lies beyond the immediate situation. This requires us to differentiate between content of a conflict and its context.

When we use presenting issues as a window we approach conflict with two lenses. One brings into focus the substance of the content, and the other seeks to see in and through the content, to the nature of the context and relational patterns. This approach calls us to differentiate between what some have called the symptomatic content of a crisis and the underpinning emotional process.[3]

This ability to look at, as well as through, permits us to develop a change-oriented process that is responsive to the immediate content and addresses the greater context within which it was given birth.

Practice 2:
Develop a capacity to integrate multiple time frames

The capacity to see through the window of the immediate situation assumes a second important discipline: the ability to think and act without being bound by the constraints of a short-term view of time. This does not mean that we think long-term simply to prevent or correct the shortsightedness of working in a crisis mentality. Rather, it means to create strategies that integrate short-term response with long-term change; we must be short-term responsive and long-term strategic.

This approach requires processes with a variety of time frames. It is important to be able to be comfortable with this multiplicity of time lines.

One specific tool that helps develop this capacity is to visualize time as connected to specific needs at different levels. A system-wide change process that addresses the culture of an organization—for example, how departments will be re-conceived and coordinated within an organization in order to reflect a new mission statement—may need to be thought about as a multi-year process. Who will be responsible for working Saturdays during this next year while the discussions are ongoing? This need requires a short-term, immediate process that produces clear, workable solutions to a specific problem.

If people can see what, when, and why things are happening, if they have a visual time frame that integrates and delineates the types of processes and the time provided for dealing with each one of them, then they can more easily comprehend the idea of immediate problem-solving and longer-range strategic change.

The transformation-oriented practitioner must cultivate the capacity to recognize what sorts of process-related time frames may be necessary to address the different kinds of change required.

Practice 3:

Develop the capacity to pose
the energies of conflict as dilemmas

I tend to link two ideas with the phrases "and at the same time." This is not just a quirk in my writing; it has become part of my way of thinking and formulating perspective. It reflects my effort to shift my thinking from an either/or to a both/and frame of reference. This is what I would call the art and discipline of posing conflicts as dilemmas.

This approach initially emerged for me in settings of deeply rooted, violent conflict. Very difficult issues were demanding immediate attention and choices. The decisions we faced seemed to pose outright contradictions as framed by the people involved and even by ourselves as practitioners. For example, those of us working in relief and aid agencies in Somalia in the early 1990s struggled daily with overwhelming decisions in the middle of a disastrous war, drought, and famine. We were faced with choices about where to put our energies and responses when none of the apparent options seemed adequate. Should we send in food and relief aid even though we knew armed groups took advantage of it to continue the war, which was itself one of the key reasons why a famine existed and relief was needed? Or should we not send food, in order to avoid unintentionally contributing to the fighting, and instead work on peace initiatives, knowing that we would feel helpless about the enormous humanitarian plight? Far too often the way we posed our questions limited our strategies.

When we changed our way of framing questions to "both and," our thinking shifted. We learned to recognize the legitimacy of different, but not incompatible, goals and energies within the conflict setting. Rather than accepting a frame of reference that placed our situation as choosing between competing energies, we reframed the questions to hold both at the same time. How can we build capacities for peace in this setting *and at the same time* create responsive mechanisms for the delivery of humanitarian aid? The very formulation of the question creates a capacity to recognize the underlying energies and to develop integrative processes and responses that hold them together.

When we embrace dilemmas and paradoxes, there is the possibility that in conflict we are not dealing with outright incompatibilities. Rather, we are faced with recognizing and responding to different but interdependent aspects of a complex situation. We are not able to handle complexity well if we understand our choices in rigid either/or and contradictory terms. Complexity requires that we develop the capacity to identify the key energies in a situation and hold them up together as **interdependent goals.**

A simple formula provides us entry into the world of dilemmas and paradoxes. Its application in real time and real-life situations requires a great deal of discipline, repetition, and creativity. The formula is this: How can we address "A" and at the same time build "B"?

The ability to position situations as dilemmas, the capacity to live with apparent contradictions and paradoxes, lies at the heart of transformation. The art of dilemma-posing creates a simple way to see the bigger picture and to move us toward specific action.

Dilemmas imply complexity. This view suggests the ability to live with and to see the value of complexity.

Further, it requires us to resist the push to resolve everything rationally into neat, logically consistent packages. This suggests another capacity that often needs to be cultivated.

Practice 4:

Develop a capacity to make complexity a friend, not a foe

In conflicts, especially when there has been a long history of patterns and episodes that were not constructively addressed, people feel overwhelmed. You hear phrases like, "This situation is such a mess. It is just too complicated. There are too many things going on to even try to explain it." These are the signs and voices of complexity raising its head. The challenge to conflict transformation is how to make complexity a friend rather than a foe.

The capacity to live with apparent contradictions and paradoxes lies at the heart of transformation.

At times of escalated conflict, complexity describes a situation in which we feel forced to live with multiple and competing frames of reference about what things mean. We are faced with a lot happening at multiple levels between different sets of people, all at the same time. Complexity suggests multiplicity and simultaneity. By its very nature, complexity in conflict creates an atmosphere of rising ambiguity and uncertainty. Things are not clear. We feel insecure about the meaning of all that is happening, we are not sure where it is going, and we feel as if we have little or no control over what happens. No wonder we see complexity as a foe creating an interminable headache. No wonder we often believe that simplifying the issues or resolving the contradictions will bring remedy.

We all have a certain tolerance for complexity, but we all reach our point of saturation. When saturated, some of us cope by leaving, by getting out. Others of us stay but try to find a quick fix or solution that makes the complexity go away. Still others of us try to reduce the impact by ignoring the multiple meanings and faces. We settle on a single explanation about what is going on, then hold onto it doggedly and rigidly. Complexity becomes the enemy.

Paradoxically, as Abraham Lincoln observed, "The only way to truly get rid of an enemy is to make him your friend." While complexity can create a sense that there is too much to consider, it also provides untold possibilities for building desired and constructive change. One of the great advantages of complexity is that change is not tied exclusively to one thing, one action, one option. In fact, complexity can create the feeling of being a kid in a candy store: we are not limited by having too few options but by our own inability to experience the wide range of potentials afforded by all the available choices.

The key to this fourth practice is to trust and pursue but never to be rigid. First, we must trust the capacity of systems to generate options and avenues for change and moving forward. Second, we must pursue those that appear to hold the greatest promise for constructive change. Third, we must not lock rigidly onto one idea or avenue.

Complexity often brings a multiplicity of options to the surface. If we pay careful attention to those options, we can often create new ways to look at old patterns.

Practice 5:

Develop a capacity to hear and engage the voices of identity

I have repeatedly suggested that we should look for and see the patterns in the context underpinning the presenting situation, in the epicenter of the conflict. But what do we look and listen for? I have consistently found that most essential is hearing and engaging the struggling, sometimes lost, voices of identity within the loud static of the conflictive environment. In my experience, issues of identity are at the root of most conflicts. Thus a capacity to understand and respect the role of identity is essential to understanding the epicenter of conflict.

Issues of identity are fundamental in protecting a sense of self and group survival, and they become particularly important during conflicts. Identity shapes and moves an expression of conflict, often in terms of deeply felt demands and preferred outcomes, to presenting issues. At the deepest level, identity is lodged in the narratives of how people see themselves, who they are, where they have come from, and what they fear they will become or lose. Thus, identity is deeply rooted in a person's or a group's sense of how that person or group is in relationship with others and what effect that relationship has on its participants' sense of self and group. Identity matters are fundamental to conflict, yet they are rarely explicitly addressed in the conflict.

Identity is not a rigid, static phenomenon. Rather, identity is dynamic and under constant definition and redefinition, especially during times of conflict. Identity is also best understood as relational. If we had no other color in the world than the color blue, then blue would be colorless. To distinguish blue we need a matrix of colors; then "blue" in relationship has identity and makes sense.

This creates a challenge for a transformational process: how do we create spaces and processes that encourage people to address and articulate a positive sense of identity in relationship to other people and groups, but not in reaction to them? In the middle of conflict, when people are often filled with great fears and unknowns, the challenge is to lower the level of reactivity and blame, while at the same time increasing a capacity to express a clear sense of self and place.

What are the disciplines that make such a practice possible?

First, we need to develop a capacity to see and hear "identity" when it appears. Be attentive to language, metaphors, and expressions that signal the distresses of identity. Sometimes these are vague: "Five years ago, not one teacher in this school would have thought of proposing such a course. What are we coming to?" Sometimes it is named by "insider" metaphor and language: "The Pioneer Street people no longer even have a voice in this church." (Pioneer Street is where the church is located, but it is also the inside label for the first-generation members of the church). Sometimes it is explicit and mobilized: "The very survival of the Hmong community is under threat by the actions of this Police Chief." In all cases, pay attention to the concern behind the voice. It is an appeal to a sense of self, to identity, and to how a relationship is being experienced and defined. It is an appeal to take the discourse from the content to the core. You cannot touch the epicenter if you do not hear the voice. The first step: be attentive to the voice of identity.

Second, move toward, not away from, the appeals to identity. Acknowledge that the conflict requires us to address our understandings of identity and relationship. This does not take the place of a process which needs to be designed to address the specific issues and content that surfaced the conflict. Both processes are needed. Generating solutions to specific problems can alleviate anxiety temporarily, but it rarely addresses deeper identity and relational concerns directly.

Processes designed to explore these deeper issues will need to have a goal of creating spaces for exchange and dialogue, rather than the goal of creating an immediate negotiated solution. Also, in working with identity-based concerns it is important not to assume that the work is primarily that of direct inter-identity exchange. Often the most critical parts of the process are the cultivation of internal, self, or intra-group spaces, where safe and deep reflection about the nature of the situation, responsibility, hopes, and fears can be pursued.

Pushing inappropriately for inter-identity exchange without a framework of preparation and adequate support can be counterproductive and even destructive. When working with identity, I can suggest three guiding principles that should characterize the process: honesty, iterative learning, and appropriate exchange.

Honesty can never be forced. We can, however, work toward the creation of process and spaces where people feel safe enough to be deeply honest with themselves and with others about their fears and hopes, hurts and responsibilities. Cycles and episodes of escalated conflict create and reinforce an environment of insecurity that threatens identity. In turn, a threat to identity creates a tendency toward self-protection, which, while not the enemy of honesty, tends to diminish self-reflective honesty in favor of other-reflective honesty: I see clearly and honestly what is wrong with *you*. I cannot see so clearly and honestly my own responsibility. Deep honesty comes hand in hand with safety and trust. Give constant attention to how the processes are creating and assuring spaces with these characteristics.

The phrase *"iterative learning"* suggests an idea of going around. To iterate is to repeat. It requires rounds of interaction. This is especially true for issues of identity.

The questions "Who am I?" and "Who are we?" are foundational for understanding life and community. Yet speaking deeply about self, group, and relationship is never easy or elemental. Nor is identity rigid and fixed. Understanding and defining identity requires rounds of interaction and inner action. The development, negotiation, and definition of identity require processes of interaction with others, as well as inner reflection

Try never to ignore or talk away someone's perception. Instead, try to understand where it is rooted.

about self. The whole undertaking is a learning process. And the pace of learning can be very different from one person to the next. This is important because we must recognize that identity work is not a one-time decision-making process. It is an iterative process of learning, and it is done in relationship to others.

Those who support or facilitate transformational processes therefore need to think about how to create multiple forums for addressing identity. Too often we think of the transaction as a one-time event that deals with identity and then is over. Instead, it is better to see process as a platform that permits ongoing learning about self and other, while at the same time pursuing decisions about particular issues that symbolize the deeper negotiations surrounding identity. This is why, for example, conflict transformation views the dispute over a parade in Belfast or Portadown, Northern Ireland, as simultaneously an issue requiring specific decisions related to that episode and an iterative platform to explore and shape identities of people with shared childhoods and geographic horizons. You can use the episodic issue as an opportunity to explore identity, but you cannot use the limited time and scope of the decision-making process about a specific issue as an adequate mechanism for addressing identity concerns.

As we seek appropriate forms of interaction or exchange, we can easily fall into a technique-oriented approach toward dialogue and assume that it can only happen in direct face-to-face processes. Appropriate exchange suggests there are many ways that learning and deepening understanding about identity and relationship can happen. We need not fall prey to "process" overload that suggests "dialogue-as-talk" is the only path to understanding. In deep identity work the opposite may be true. Appropriate exchange may include dialogue through music, the arts, rituals, dialogue-as-sport, fun and laughter, and dialogue-as-shared-work to preserve old city centers or parks. All of these may have greater avenues for learning and understanding than talk can possibly provide. The key to this fifth capacity is an ability to recognize opportunity and to design response processes with innovation and creativity.

Finally, we need to be attentive to peoples' perceptions of how identity is linked to power and to the systems and structures which organize and govern their relationships. This is particularly important for people who feel their identity has historically been eroded, marginalized, or under deep threat. Here change processes must address the ways in which structural relationships symbolize and represent the perceptions. The key: try never to ignore or talk away someone's perception. Instead, try to understand where it is rooted. Never propose or tinker with structural arrangements as a tactic to avoid the deeper perception. When dealing with identity-based concerns encourage participants to be honest as they look at and address systemic changes, which they need in order to assure them both respect and access to the structures.

Practices such as these are not natural skills for many of us. They take commitment and discipline, but when developed they increase our capacity to think and respond transformatively to conflict.

9.
Applying the Framework

I am sitting in a coffeehouse in the town where I live in Colorado, next to several people who are in an animated, sometimes heated, discussion about a rising controversy with local police. The town's newspaper has been filled these past two months with letters to the editor deploring recent policing actions. The police seem to have decided that speeding and rolling stops require much more attention.

At the table next to me the voices rise as one person details her recent experience of getting a ticket for speeding. She explains that she had not been stopped in 20 years, and she is convinced that the current drive is just a ploy to fill the town coffers. She concludes with a lament about the loss of citizenship in what used to be a friendly town. A few weeks ago a protest march was organized on Main Street, followed by a public forum to air grievances and to decide on the next steps.

This is not the first time controversy has arisen around the police. Four years ago the main complaint in the papers was that the police were too slow in responding to calls for help, especially in an area where out-of-state people were starting illegal campfires. Last year the letters to the editor carried wide-ranging views about police personnel issues and what should or should not be done about a recent firing. I overheard one friend of the police comment, "Some say they move too slow. Some say they are too worried about speed. They must be about right." That remark was not well received by the person who had just gotten a ticket.

In the stories at the coffeehouse, the protest march slogans, and the letters to the editor we can see the elements discussed in the preceding chapters. How would a transformational view look at this controversy? What might a platform for conflict transformation look like in response? Let's imagine, in *Little Book* fashion, what our lenses would pick up and suggest.

1. What do our lenses bring into focus?

Episode lenses suggest:
- A recent time frame—the past few months—has seen the rise of controversy, and increased community attention to and tension around the police, and this needs to be addressed.
- The content is about specific kinds of actions and behaviors. In this episode, it is about tickets for speeding and a pattern of stopping certain kinds of people.
- The relational grievance has to do with how individuals have been treated when stopped.

Epicenter lenses suggest:
- This is not the first time the community and police have had controversies. There is a repeated pattern of episodes on a variety of different content issues.
- Relational patterns are expressed in the way individuals and police have interacted over time.

- Structural patterns are expressed in how the community views the role, responsibilities, and expectations of policing, and how police and town officials view the responsibility of providing security.
- Identity patterns are expressed in how citizens, governing officials, and police view the town, the kind of town each wants, and how policing fits the image of who we were in the past and who we want to be in the future.
- Interdependence, and power patterns embedded in the relationships, are expressed in expectations and frustrations, fears and hopes about how citizens and governing structures relate, make decisions, and include (or exclude) citizens in decisions that affect their lives.

2. What questions do these lenses raise?
Episode suggests:
- Can we do something about the number of seemingly unwarranted stops that are being made for speeding?
- Can we improve the way police treat local citizens when they do stop them?
- Can we agree on what citizens' responsibilities are for safe driving in a small town with a lot of pedestrians?
- Can we understand the mandate for safety as determined by law that the police are helping to uphold and ultimately are responsible to apply?

Epicenter suggests:
- Can we discuss and develop a bill of rights and responsibilities of and for local police and citizens that prevents abuse and promotes safety?

- Can we create a longer-term vision of what our town needs in terms of policing? What should the police department's mission and role be? How it is responsive to the kind of town we want to be and the needs we have?
- Can we establish a mechanism that provides citizens a voice in raising concerns and provides a regular and routine way of having constructive interaction between the police and the citizenry?

Posing a dilemma asks:
- How can we address the issue of speeding and other safety infractions *and at the same time* design processes that facilitate the development of a common vision for community policing?
- How can we address the needs for safety and security in town *while at the same time* providing mechanisms for addressing citizen and police duties and responsibilities that match the needs and expectations of local citizens, police, and governing officials?

3. What would a transformational platform suggest?
 a. The episode has created energy to do something touching a wider citizenry. This has become an opportunity to explore the potential of what is good for the whole community. So we must not look exclusively at the presenting issues. Instead, we must take a view that looks back across the patterns of the past five, 10, maybe even 20 years. Let the issues be a window into the relational context that is a backdrop to this community, and then come back to look at the design of processes.

b. We need processes that respond both to the immediate issues and the longer-term agenda. The presenting issues are a good window into the nature of the repeated patterns. They suggest some avenues for what may be useful in the future. Let's think about multiple processes, each with different time frame requirements, but ones that are linked. Examples of such processes might include:

i. A facilitated community forum to air grievances and clarify immediate needs and solutions.

ii. A facilitated community forum to talk about expectations for community policing.

iii. An initiative to develop regular exchange and feedback between police and citizens.

iv. An initiative to develop a facilitated long-range strategic plan for establishing a mission statement and guiding values for policing, involving both citizens, police, and town officials.

v. A plan to initiate a citizen-police advisory panel that creates specific ways citizens and police can consult and exchange their concerns, hopes, and fears.

It is important to note that each of these, although they may be thought about and launched simultaneously, require different kinds of support structures and time frames as they are carried out. Some may be a one-time event, some are ongoing processes, and still others may, in fact, become new community structures and resources. Remember, we are thinking about change processes and what facilitates constructive change.

c. In proposing the process of response to the immediate situation, think about whether there may be ways to build a new and ongoing response mechanism for concerns about policing. For example, an advisory or facilitative group, as proposed above, might initially be seen as the way to work with the immediate process, but they could also become a facilitative mechanism for ongoing community response on longer-range issues. The idea is this: We can expect new episodes in the future given the patterns of the past. Can we establish something that helps us to prepare and respond more constructively? This type of mechanism would become, in fact, a new social space, a structure, and it needs to be made up of people who are not like-minded and who are from different parts of the community. It would likely be initiated informally and take on a more formal role if it is deemed to be useful. If it works well in the future, it becomes an ongoing platform of response to emerging situations, both preventing and facilitating.

d. The design should include a forum for discussing current issues and the capacity to continue discussing. However, the processes should not rely exclusively on "talk" as the only mechanism for dialogue. We must think carefully about community processes, events, and common initiatives where there might naturally be constructive interaction between police and community that can be built on over the next number of years.

So what happened in the real life situation? The story is not yet over. It never is. But some interesting features did develop. Several good facilitated community forums and discussions were created. Some dynamic people from the police department and a number of concerned citizens reached out constructively to the other side. A proposed advisory panel on policing appears to be emerging and taking shape. These signs suggest that the episode may have created a window into the epicenter. Solutions have been initiated for the immediate problems, and it may be that changes in the relational and identity patterns are under development. Check back in five years. Meanwhile, you might want to try out these lenses, questions, and platforms in your hometown.

10.
Conclusions

The lenses of conflict transformation raise questions for participants and practitioners that emphasize the potential for constructive change inherent in conflict. These lenses can be applied to many kinds of conflicts; the potential of broader desired change is inherent in any episode of conflict, from personal to structural levels. The challenge before the practitioner is to assess whether the circumstances merit investment in designing a tranformational response to a particular situation.

A key advantage within this framework lies in its capacity to consider multiple avenues of response. I have suggested that transformation builds from and integrates the contribution and strengths of conflict resolution approaches. But conflict resolution does not necessarily incorporate the transformative potential of conflict. In other words, you can use a transformational approach and conclude that the most appropriate thing to do is a quick and direct resolution of the problem, period. But conflict resolution narrowly defined does not automatically raise the questions and inquiries necessary to spark the potential for broader change.

Clearly, a transformative approach is more appropriate in some situations than others. There are many conflicts or disputes where a simple resolution approach such as problem-solving or negotiation makes the most sense. Disputes that involve the need for a quick and final solution to a problem, where the disputants have little or no relationship before, during, or after, are clearly situations in which the exploration of relational and structural patterns are of limited value. For example, a one-time business dispute over a payment between two people who hardly know each other and will never have contact again is not a setting for exploring a transformational application. At best, if it were applied, the primary focus might be on the patterns of why these people as individuals have this episode, and whether the episode repeats itself time and again with other people.

On the other hand, where there are significant past relationships and history, where there are likely to be significant future relationships, where the episodes arise in an organizational, community, or broader social context—here the narrowness of resolution approaches may solve problems but miss the greater potential for constructive change. This is especially important in contexts where there are repeated and deep-rooted cycles of conflict episodes that have created destructive and violent patterns. From the perspective of conflict transformation, these are always situations where the potential for change can be raised.

> The narrowness of resolution approaches may solve problems but miss the greater potential for constructive change.

In any situation, however, the decision of whether to pursue all the potential avenues of change must be assessed and weighed. Our family does not engage in a deep transformational exploration every time we have an argument about dirty dishes. But over periods of time there are episodes that do create the circumstances for deeper reflection about our patterns, the structure of our relationship, and our identity as individuals and as a family. The dirty dishes always hold the potential. We don't pursue it on every occasion. But if and when we want to pursue it, the potential can only be opened if we have a framework that encourages the inquiry, provides lenses to see what is happening, and offers tools to help us think about constructive change. That framework is what conflict transformation offers.

Perhaps most importantly, conflict transformation places before us the big questions: Where are we headed? Why do we do this work? What are we hoping to contribute and build? I am convinced that the vast majority of practitioners who have chosen to work in this field are drawn to it because they want to promote social change. I am convinced that most of the communities who have committed to finding constructive ways to address conflict are likewise interested, not just in maintaining the status quo, but in changing lives for the better. They want to change the way human societies respond to conflict. The change these practitioners and communities desire is to move from violent and destructive patterns toward capacities which are creative, responsive, constructive, and nonviolent.

I am one of those practitioners, and perhaps my biases cause me to see what I wish to see. I see that our human community, local and global, is on the edge of historic change where patterns of violence and coercion will be replaced with respect, creative problem-solving, individual and social capacities for dialogue, and nonvi-

Conclusions

olent systems for assuring human security and social change. This will require a complex web of change processes guided by a transformational understanding of life and relationship. This is my challenge and hope for conflict transformation.

> May the warmth of complexity shine on your face.
> May the winds of good change blow gently
>   at your back.
> May your feet find the roads of authenticity.
> May the web of change begin!

Endnotes

[1] The New Sciences are the developments in physics, biology, and environmental studies that in the latter half of the 20th century produced quantum and chaos theories, among others.

See Margaret Wheatley's discussion of this in reference to learning organizations in *Leadership and the New Sciences* (San Francisco, CA: Barrett-Koehler, Publishers, 1994) p. 16.

[2] Ibid.

[3] See Hocker and Wilmot's discussion of content and relationship in *Interpersonal Conflict* or Edwin Friedman's discussion of anxiety, emotional process, and symptomatic content in *Generation to Generation*.

Selected Readings

Bush, Baruch and J. Folger. *The Promise of Mediation: Responding to Conflict Through Empowerment and Recognition* (San Francisco: Jossey-Bass, 1994).

Curle, Adam. *Another Way: Positive Response to Contemporary Violence* (Oxford: Jon Carpenter Publishing, 1995).

Friedman, Edwin. *Generation to Generation: Family Process in Church and Synagogue* (New York: Guilford Press, 1985).

Hocker, Joyce and William Wilmot. *Interpersonal Conflict* (Dubuque: Brown and Benchmark, 2000).

Kriesberg, Louis. *Constructive Conflicts: From Escalation to Resolution. Second Edition* (New York: Rowman and Littlefield Publishers, 2003).

Mayer, Bernard. *The Dynamics of Conflict Resolution: A Practitioner's Guide* (San Francisco: Jossey-Bass, 2000).

Rothman, Jay. *Resolving Identity-Based Conflicts in Nations, Organizations and Communities* (San Francisco: Jossey-Bass, 1997).

Ury, Bill. *The Third Side: Why we fight and how we can stop* (New York: Penguin, 2000).

Wehr, Paul and Heidi and Guy Burgess. *Justice without Violence* (Boulder: Lynne Riener, 1994).

Wheatley, Margaret. *Leadership and the New Science: Learning about organization from an orderly universe* (San Francisco: Berrett-Koehler, 1994).

Related Books by John Paul Lederach

Preparing for Peace: Conflict Transformation Across Cultures (Syracuse University Press, 1995).

Building Peace: Sustainable Reconciliation in Divided Societies (U.S. Institute of Peace Press, 1997).

The Journey Toward Reconciliation (Herald Press, 1999).

From the Ground Up: Mennonite Contributions to International Peacebuidling, edited with Cynthia Sampson (Oxford University Press, 2000).

Into the Eye of the Storm: A Handbook of International Peacebuilding (Jossey-Bass, 2002).

About the Author

John Paul Lederach is Professor of International Peacebuilding at the Joan B. Kroc Institute of International Peace Studies, University of Notre Dame, and a Distinguished Scholar with the Center for Justice and Peacebuilding at Eastern Mennonite University. He has worked in the fields of conflict transformation and peacebuilding for more than 20 years. He works extensively in support of international conciliation efforts in Latin America, Asia, Africa, and Central Asia, as well as in North America. He has authored and co-edited 15 books and manuals in English and Spanish.

Dr. Lederach received his Ph.D. in Sociology (with a concentration in the Social Conflict Program) from the University of Colorado.

Lederach and his wife, Wendy, have two children, Angie and Josh.

Group Discounts for

The Little Book of
Conflict Transformation
ORDER FORM

If you would like to order multiple copies of *The Little Book of Conflict Transformation* for groups you know or are a part of, please email **bookorders@skyhorsepublishing.com** or fax order to **(212) 643-6819**. (Discounts apply only for more than one copy.)

Photocopy this page and the next as often as you like.

The following discounts apply:

1 copy	$5.99
2-5 copies	$5.39 each (a 10% discount)
6-10 copies	$5.09 each (a 15% discount)
11-20 copies	$4.79 each (a 20% discount)
21-99 copies	$4.19 each (a 30% discount)
100 or more	$3.59 each (a 40% discount)

Free Shipping for orders of 100 or more!

Prices subject to change.

Quantity   *Price*   *Total*

The Little Book of

____ copies of *Conflict Transformation* @ _____ _____

(Standard ground shipping costs will be added for orders of less than 100 copies.)

METHOD OF PAYMENT

❒   Check or Money Order
       (*payable to **Skyhorse Publishing** in U.S. funds*)

❒   Please charge my:
❒ MasterCard ❒ Visa
❒ Discover   ❒ American Express

\# _____

Exp. date and sec. code_____

Signature _____

Name _____

Address _____

City_____

State _____

Zip_____

Phone_____

Email _____

SHIP TO: (if different)
Name _____

Address _____

City_____

State _____

Zip_____

Call: (212) 643-6816
Fax: (212) 643-6819
Email: bookorders@skyhorsepublishing.com
(do not email credit card info)